HELL QUIZZES TO A STREET PREACHER

All around us today we hear non-Catholics declaring that, "There is no Hell," "Hell is a myth," "Intellectual progress has abolished Hell." Prof. G. H. Betts, of the Northwestern University in his book "The Belief of 700 Ministers," shows in his tabulations of replies received from 500 ministers and 200 Protestant theological schools, in 20 denominations that 13 per cent were uncertain of Hell's existence, and 34 per cent **disbelieved or denied** the existence of Hell. As a conclusion to his findings he says, **"No denomination except perhaps the Lutherans has any right to demand that fixed creeds shall be taught their young."**

The following questions and statements to a radio and street preacher are samples of what the so-called Reformation has done for the modern mind:

1. I don't like Hell.

Who does like Hell? The fact that you don't like Hell doesn't prove that it is all humbug. Diderot, a rationalist, set down in his notes a little self-interrogation, "If you abuse your reason, my soul, you will not only be unhappy in this life, but still more unhappy in Hell."

"And who told you that there is a Hell?"

"Well, even if it be doubtful, you had better live as if there were one."

"What if I am sure there is no Hell?"

"I defy you to prove it."

Voltaire replied in the same strain to a friend who wrote to him, "I believe that I have at last found certainty that no Hell exists at all."

"Lucky man," wrote back Voltaire, "I am very far yet from that."

Still, many people choose not to believe in Hell, and in order to pat themselves on the back to give themselves confidence they assert no one really believes that ancient doctrine of priestcraft. There are 431,000,000 members of the Catholic Church who believe that ancient but still modern doctrine.

2. What do you mean by Hell?

Though the modernized man jokes about Hell, scoffs at it, doubts and denies it, Hell is the eternal lot of misery awaiting those who die in a state of grave sin and at enmity with God. Before the general resurrection, the soul alone experiences this misery; after the resurrection, the body will be reunited with that soul and will share in the misery, being tormented by created elements even as the person forsook God during life for the enjoyment of created things. The chief misery will be the sense of having lost happiness of the Vision of God; the other will be the torment of fire.

3. If you believe in Hell, you believe that it is necessary for others, but not for yourselves.

No Catholic believes that anyone necessarily goes to Hell. No man need go there at all. But if a man separates himself from God by sin and dies in a state of mortal or grave sin, he has fixed his state forever and will go to Hell; and this is truth which every Catholic admits as applicable to himself as well as to all other human beings.

4. Catholics cannot genuinely believe in Hell.

Catholics genuinely believe in the existence of Hell. I believe in it and I have not the most attenuated shadow of a doubt as to the existence of Hell. Nor has any other practical Catholic in this world. Pope, Cardinals, Bishops, priests and laymen all have this same faith, and sincerely.

5. No sane intellect could assimilate so horrible a doctrine.

Sane reason does not demand unbelief. Human intelligence cannot fully comprehend the mystery of eternal suffering, but that does not alter the fact that Hell exists, even as our not fully comprehending the medium of wireless transmission does not alter the fact that some such medium does exist. And if the thought of Hell is horrible, the thought that there is **no Hell** is still more horrible. Grave sin against the Creator is a more horrible thing than the Hell to which it leads. And that a creature could mock its Creator with impunity is more horrible than the punishment such conduct deserves.

6. Catholics must hate the doctrine of Hell.

They do not hate the doctrine of Hell, for they love the truth as revealed by God. Then, too, this doctrine is the vindication of God's justice, and it is not possible to hate the doctrine that God is justice itself. Catholics dislike the state of Hell of course; and hate the thought of anyone going there. But the doctrine they gladly accept.

7. No wonder Catholics live by fear, whilst Protestants have such childlike love and trust in God.

What do you mean by "fear"? Do you mean servile, cringing fear, or that filial reverent fear which Scripture declares to be the beginning of wisdom? And what do you mean by "childlike love and trust"? Do you mean the repeating of the formula, "Believe in Christ and be saved," and then going on with all kinds of things which God forbids? With hosts of Protestants, "childlike love and trust are matters of vague sentiment and self-persuasion, due to ignorance even of God's just demands and revealed doctrines. As, for example, when Protestant clergymen say to their people, "There is not really a Hell. No one can tell me that there is really a Hell." Why do they preach about Heaven and have they been really informed about Heaven? And, although God **does** tell us that there is a Hell, their poor people clutch at the thought fathered by their wish and regard it as childlike love and trust to deny what God has revealed. Finally, remember that real filial and reverent fear of God, such as is instilled into Catholics, in no way excludes genuine love of God and trust in Him. These are the true wisdom to which filial fear leads.

8. I admire Catholicism but I could never sincerely believe in Hell.

You could, if you had the faith which Catholics possess, namely, that the Catholic Church, which teaches this doctrine, has the commission, protection and authority of God, in matters of religion and moral conduct, to teach, guide, and rule the souls of men.

9. Could one become a Catholic without believing in Hell?

No. But you really make an impossible supposition. He who refuses to believe in any one authoritative teaching of Christianity could not possibly have perfect faith in any others. He might have immense confidence in his own opinion as to their truth. But that is not Christian faith. He believes the other doctrines, because he likes them, and refuses to believe this because he does not approve of it. That is not Christian faith. Faith accepts a thing as true on the authority of another.

If I have faith in Christ, I believe that He knows the truth and would not tell a lie. Whatever He says I accept —whether I fully comprehend it or not because refusal to accept accuses Him of ignorance or want of veracity or want of authority. Deny any one thing Christ teaches and you deny faith in His knowledge and authority to teach. **That** motive having gone overboard, what do you accept?

You accept, not by faith in Christ or in His Church, but through confidence in your own powers of discernment. That might do, if you wish to be a disciple of yourself; but it will not do as a qualification to be a disciple of Christ and of the Catholic Church. It is all or nothing. If a man has Catholic faith, he accepts the teaching of the Catholic Church. If he will not accept her teaching, he has not received the gift of Catholic faith, and cannot become a Catholic until he does so.

10. What is the nature of Hell?

Hell is a state of eternal misery. Death in Hell would be a great mercy, only there is no death. There is but suffering, and an unending suffering in Hell. It is a departure from all that is good, holy, and beautiful. The misery of the privation of God is in proportion to the joy of the possession of God. The lost soul goes to remorse, suffering, and despair. There will be the remorse of eternal remembrance; not repentance, but consuming regret and degradation, regret that he should have to suffer thus; the degradation of his identification with sin. He is not so much in the act of sin as in the state of sin. Sin is, as it were, **humanized** in him. And consciousness of sin will come into its own. First sins bring fear and remorse to the timorous, shy, and pure conscience of a child. But men grow out of their conscience, and live it down. But what if the child conscience could knock at the heart of the grown man? And what if conscience were revived, and a man could get rid of neither his sins nor his conscience for all eternity? We can at least conceive of a **mental Hell** based on such a consideration.

But there is also a physical Hell of fire. There **is** a fire of Hell. It is not fire as we know it, for it is worse. Fire as we know it was but the nearest thing Christ could find to describe the sense-pains of Hell. And the soul will go to this remorse and suffering in utter despair. Our future is attractive so long as there is hope of some sort. If hope goes, there is only the despair of suicide. Only in Hell there is **no suicide.** "I am lost forever," is the conclusive cry of a soul, made for happiness, yet never to attain it.

11. It is simply impossible. It cannot be.

Me **must** believe in such a Hell, or give up being Christians. If there is an **up,** there must be a **down;** if there is a right, there must be a left; if there is reward, there must be punishment; if there is a Heaven, there must be a Hell. If we reject Hell, we reject the authority of God, reject the redemption and the cross; and, indeed, the whole majestic edifice of Christian faith, the source of life and true civilization, the one divine religion in this world today.

12. What evidence have you that such a Hell exists?

The very best. The God who made us tells us that He also has made a Hell. There is a Hell in which both the bodies and the souls of the lost will be afflicted. Thus the gentle Christ Himself warns us, "It is expedient for thee that one of thy members should perish rather than that thy whole body go into Hell." Matt. V, 30. Remember that all shall rise some day, the good and bad alike, the body sharing in the fate of the soul. "All that are in the graves shall hear the voice of the Son of God. And they that have done good things shall come forth unto the resurrection of life; but they that have done evil unto the resurrection of judgment." Jn. V., 29. Those who are lost will go to everlasting fire. Christ called it "Unquenchable fire." Mk. IX., 44. He tells us of the grim sentence, "Depart from me you cursed into everlasting fire which was prepared for the devil and his angels." Matt. XXV., 41. Such a solemn utterance of the judicial sentence demands the literal sense. Judges do not speak in metaphors at such moments. "Let him be hanged—but of course only metaphorically." And it will be conscious suffering. Our Lord says, "Their worm dieth not, and the fire is not extinguished." Mk. IX., 43. And again, "There shall be weeping and gnashing of teeth." Matt. XIII., 50. Continued conscious suffering is the fate of the lost. And reason demands such fate. When a man sins gravely, he chooses between God and a thing forbidden by God. He cannot have both, and he prefers to renounce God rather than the created good. If he dies without repentance his will is still alienated from God. He would do the same thing again if he got the chance. And as long as these dispositions last, he must do without God and happiness. These dispositions lasting forever once this probationary life is over, so will the penalty.

13. I have read my Bible twice from cover to cover and I find nothing about your horrible doctrine.

When you read your Bible you must have read with the pretense of a seeing blind man. Open your Bible and examine this abundant testimony: Psalms X, 7, XVII, 6, XX, 10, CXIV, 3; Judith XVI, 20-21; Job XX, 18, 22, 26, XXI 13; Wisdom XVI 16-19; Ecclesiasticus VII 19, XVI 7, XXI 10; Isaias V 4, XXVI 11, XXXIII 11-12, XLVII 14, LXV 5, LXVI 24; Jeremias XV 14; Baruch IV 35; Ezekiel XV 6-7, XX 47; Matthew III 10, 12, V 22, 29, VII 19, X28, XI 23, XIII 20, 42, 50, XVIII 8-9, XXIII 33, XXV 41; Mark IX 42, 43, 44, 45, 46, 47, 48; Luke III 9, 17, X 15, XII 5, XVI 22; John XV 6; II Peter III 7; Apocalypse XVII 16, XIX 20, XX 9, 14, 15, XXI 8.

14. My reason absolutely rejects the idea of an eternal Hell.

Your reason may not be able to comprehend the full import of the doctrine. But reason cannot refuse to acknowledge a fact revealed by God. Reason itself says that God must know, and that He could not reveal falsehood. And reason itself should tell you that your intelligence is given you that you may obey and serve God, not to enable you to set yourself up as His judge.

15. But if I were God, I would never have made a Hell.

If God were you, then, He might not have made a Hell. But God is not you. He is God. What you would do is no indication of what God must necessarily do. Even if you look round the world you do see, there are hundreds of things which do not meet with your approval. Yet God has permitted them. And if you are so far out in the world you do see, what certainty have you that your ideas of what the next world should be like have any more value?

16. This threat of Hell defeats its own object.

The warning that there is a Hell does not defeat its own object amongst those with a right idea of the truth that it does exist, yet that it is a mystery the full understanding of which is reserved to God. Human attempts to picture Hell are symbolical, and give no adequate ideas of the reality. Nor is anyone asked to concentrate though upon his own imagined and very often false estimates of what Hell is like. We know that a state of very great and eternal misery is a fact, and a possibility for us. And a man is a fool if he does not think of the fact that persistent rejection of God merits eternal rejection by God.

17. Why preach this Hell business?

Why do you preach, "Jesus Saves," "Put on Jesus," "Believe on Jesus." From what does He save except from Hell? Wouldn't Jesus Christ, in whose crucifixion you believe, be a **fool** to have come down from Heaven only to go up upon the cross to die such a horrible death? The crucifixion is all **nonsense** if there be no Hell, from which we are to be saved. Certainly if there be no Hell from which we are to be saved, men could not go there, and we would all eventually get to Heaven, whether He died or not.

18. The Hebrew word Hell "Sheol" has no other meaning than the grave.

In Hebrew "sheol" has a very wide significance, and can refer to any state of being less than Heaven. It can mean grave, underworld, kingdom of the dead, state of the eternally lost, etc. The correct sense must be discerned from the context. This is often the case with Hebrew, which is a language with a very limited vocabulary having single words with many separate meanings rather than separate words for almost every shade of thought. The context rules out any possibility of Hell being no more than the grave. Christ speaks of a fate for men which involves "unquenchable fire," where remorse does not die, and the fire is not extinguished. No one but a fool could call Our Lord's words a suitable description of the grave. The grave is the receptacle of lifeless bodies. Jesus also declares that the Hell with which He threatens the wicked is that "prepared for the devil and his angels." The devil never had a body, nor was he buried in a grave. Nor can the words "everlasting fire" constitute a reference to the grave. Hell is everlasting, and will be experienced by the lost as a curse and a blight upon their unending existence.

19. Has not the word "everlasting" been mistranslated?

It has not. When Christ said that the wicked will go into "everlasting punishment," the Greek word used is exactly the same as that used to describe "everlasting" happiness and the "everlasting" God. Efforts to put limits to the duration of Hell would put limits to the duration of Heaven, and even to the very existence of God. As long as God is God, Hell will be Hell, with all its miseries.

20. Can reason accept the idea that the Saints, who should give us good example, find part of their pleasure in seeing the tortures of the dammed?

No. The exact condition of the Saints in Heaven is a mystery to us whilst still in this life. But if you study their own lives on earth, their heroic virtues will afford you all the good example you could wish. Meantime, the sufferings of the lost, as sufferings, do not contribute to their happiness. The positive aspect of God's justice maintained does so.

21. Do you maintain that there is a real fire in Hell?

Yes. The fire of Hell is a real and created fire, physical but not material, which will affect even the bodies of men who die at enmity with God. I grant that it will differ in various characteristics from natural fire as we know it. Christ chose the word fire as being that element best known to us which produces results most similar to the effects of the fire of Hell. Yet fire as we know it depends upon combustion. The fire of Hell will not depend upon being constantly fed with fuel, but upon God's will, the principle of all existing things. If God can will that fire should exist with the aid of fuel to which He gave its properties, He certainly can produce and conserve fire by simply willing it, and without the aid of created fuel. Thus He manifested to Moses a bush in flames yet unconsumed.

And if that fire were not real, it would be absurd to speak of consigning men to it. Christ's solemn utterance of a judicial sentence demands the literal sense. Judges do not speak in metaphors at such moments, saying, "Let him be hanged, but, of course, only metaphorically."

22. What is the nature of this fire in Hell?

The nature of the fire which will torment the lost is not of very great importance. Nor can difficulties concerning its nature prove the doctrine of Hell wrong. That we have difficulties proves no more than that we have them, and that is not in the least surprising when another world is being discussed on a basis of ideas drawn from this world. I grant that, although the fire of Hell is real, it must differ in nature from earthly fire as we know it, and that in many ways. The fire of Hell is a created reality, which Christ made known to us by choosing that element which in our experience produces results most similar to the effects of the fire of Hell.

23. If the soul alone is sent to Hell after death, could such a "real fire" roast that soul?

It is evident that it afflicts the devil, who is a purely spiritual being. "Everlasting fire," said Christ, "which was prepared for the devil and his angels." He was obviously referring to a real agent of suffering distinct from the devil and his angels. Of course, a spiritual being cannot be roasted as one roasts a chicken. But there is nothing to prevent a spiritual being from experiencing mental apprehension and actual physical pain by a created environment restricting its activities and restraining it from attaining to the possession of the happiness for which it was made. Whatever the explanation, however, the fact stands God has told us that there is a Hell. It is no argument against Hell to say, "I do not understand it." The only possible argument would be the proof that God never did reveal the doctrine. That proof no man will ever be able to produce.

24. Heb. II, 14, tells us that the Devil is to be destroyed. Who then will keep the fire of Hell going?

The text means that Christ will destroy the power of the devil over the souls of the redeemed. Satan will never be personally destroyed. And in any case he does not keep the fire of Hell going. If Satan had anything to do with it, that fire would have been destroyed long ago. He has never enjoyed it. However, the torments of Hell are dependent upon the will of God.

25. Will this fire also afflict the bodies of the lost?

After the general resurrection, yes. Christ has said, "All that are in the grave shall hear the voice of the Son of God. And they that have done good things shall come forth into the resurrection of life; but they that have done evil, unto the resurrection of judgment." (Jn. V., 28-29.) So all shall rise, good and bad alike, men's bodies sharing in the fate of the soul. And in Mt. V., 29, Christ says, grimly, not jokingly, "It is expedient for thee that one of thy members should perish rather than that thy whole body be cast into Hell." The whole man, body and soul, will either be saved, to experience the happiness of the glorified and risen Christ, or lost, to experience the miseries of Hell. Some people have the happy little habit of believing in Heaven because they like it, and denying Hell because they don't like it. But the Catholic Church teaches what Christ taught, because Christ taught it. The uncomfortable parts of Christ's teachings are not untrue because uncomfortable.

26. How many souls are lost according to the Catholic Church?

Various theologians have expressed various opinions. But these are merely private opinions. The Catholic Church has no official teaching on the subject, nor has any definite information been revealed to men by God. The one thing certain is that men can be saved and men can be lost, and that unrepented mortal sin is the deciding factor. That is enough for all practical purposes. Yet some of the Scriptural texts show us that the number of the saved, though great, is small in comparison with the lost. Mt. 20, 16, "Many are called, but few chosen." Mt. 7, 13-14, "Wide is the gate and broad is the way that leadeth to destruction, and many there are who go in thereat. How narrow is the gate and straight is the way that leadeth to Life; and few there are that find it." Lu. 13, 24. "Strive to enter by the narrow gate; for many, I say to you, shall seek to enter, and shall not be able." 1 C., 9, 24-25, "Know you not that they that run in the race, all run indeed, but one receiveth the prize? So run that you may obtain. And everyone that striveth for the mastery refraineth himself from all things; and they indeed that they may receive a corruptible crown, but we an incorruptible one."

27. Your Church will have increasing difficulty in getting intelligent men to believe in Hell.

The stream of converts from the ranks of intelligent men is sufficient answer to that suggestion. If you think the Catholic Church is the Church of the superstitious and ignorant, then examine this partial list of the many brilliant minds in the literary field alone, who have become converts to the Catholic Church:

Paul Claudel, Sheila Kay-Smith, David Goldstein, Sigrid Undset, G. K. Chesterton, Compton Mackkenzie, Alfred Noyes, Joyce Kilmer, F. Marion Crawford, Giovanni Papini, Johannes Jorgensen, Maurice Baring, Theodore Maynard, Ronald Knox, Sir Bertram Windle, Shane Leslie, Max Pemberton, John L. Stoddard, Aubrey de Vere, Robert Hugh Benson, Coventry Patmore, "Artemus Ward," Joel Chandler Harris, Michael Williams, Rose Hawthorne, "John Ayscough," Henry Harland, C. C. Martindale, Robert H. Lord, Cecil Chesterton, Selden P. Delany, Charles Warren Stoddard, Isabel Clarke, Wilfred Meynell, Enid Dennis, John Moody, Owen Dudley, Kent Stone, etc., etc.

In one category of 3,000 American converts 372 were Protestant ministers, 115 doctors, 126 lawyers, 45 former members of Congress, 12 governors of states, 180 Army and Navy Officers, and 206 authors, musicians and persons of cultural prominence. There figures were taken from "Our Sunday Visitor."

28. How can you reconcile Hell with God's love, justice and mercy?

If I could not, that would but prove something wrong with my own ideas on the subject. For it is certain that God is loving, just, and merciful; and He has revealed that there is a Hell. So the ideas cannot be repugnant. However God's love, justice, and mercy demand that there be a Hell. His love demands a Hell, for the more He loves the more He must hate sin. To the man who says that God loves too much to send a man to Hell, I simply reply that He sends no man there; men go there. And God has loved too much not to let them go there if they scorn, reject, and throw God's love back in His face. Again, His justice demands that if a man dies rejecting an infinite goodness he should endure a penalty of a never-ending nature. If there were no eternal punishment, a man could cry to God, "You say, 'Thou shalt not.' I say, 'I shall.' Do Your worst. You cannot punish me forever. What care I for Your commandments or for Yourself! You must either make me happy in the end, or annihilate me, when I shall have escaped Your power." It is impossible for the drama of iniquity to end like that. That would not be justice. And as for God's mercy, already it is a mercy that man has the thought of Hell as an emergency brake to stop his headlong rush into vice. The truth that there is a Hell has mercifully saved many a soul from a life of blasphemy and sin, and still more often from death in a state of sin. And remember that God's mercy is offered to every man over and over again during life. Mercy is asked for, not forced upon people. Some men who are loudest in their protests against God's injustice would be the first to complain if God forced anything upon them, even his mercy. But men cannot have God's mercy and reject it at one and the same time.

29. Try as I may, I cannot reconcile the idea with God's mercy.

You can safely leave that problem to God. All your speculations now will not alter conditions then. God knows best, and you can be sure that whatever He disposes will be in keeping with all His attributes, and in accordance with a far nobler and higher estimate of God than any you can form in this life. And remember that mercy is not foolishness. As a matter of fact, God offers His mercy over and over again to every soul during life. This soul cannot persevere in rejecting it, and have it. A man who leans upon God's mercy to deny the danger, and denies the danger in order to offend God still more, is but making a mockery of God's most precious attribute. Do you want God to forget that He is God, and plead forever with a creature that despises and rejects Him? Is it possible for the drama of iniquity to end like that? And if sin has turned purity into filth, humility into pride, hope into despair, and love into hate, what would such a soul do in the presence of God? Hell is the only fit place for it.

30. But Christ who came as the Revelation of God, was so kind and gentle!

That intensifies the force of the arguments for Hell. Only a grim reality could have forced Him to speak as He did. He taught Heaven and Hell equally. You cannot have Heaven because you like it and reject a Hell taught by the same authority because you do not like it. Think of His passion and death. If there were no Hell to save us from; if we all had to go to Heaven whether He were crucified or not, then His sufferings and death were foolish. Men wish to abolish Hell. There is but one way to do so. Let each man abolish his own Hell by repenting of his sins and endeavoring to serve God.

31. You make Christ cruel.

I do not. Due punishment for not doing as Christ commands is justice, not cruelty. Parents know that it is not cruelty to inflict reasonable and deserved punishment upon children who are rebellious. And God has more right to your obedience than any parents to the obedience of their children. It is a blameworthy weakness in parents if they allow their children to do just as they please with no fear of the consequences. And God is not so foolish as to give serious laws to His rational creatures on the understanding that nothing will happen if they break them. But there is no need to endure the extreme penalty. Keep the laws and you will keep safe.

32. Your Hell is full of non-Catholics, who commit grave sin and do not know how to make an act of perfect contrition.

We do not know how far they understand the gravity of sin. As for the act of contrition, you are leaving out the greatest factor of all—God's grace. In a flash God can enlighten the mind and move the will to a purely interior act of contrition of which the onlookers know nothing. And God alone knows how many are thus saved.

33. If you believe in Christianity you must believe that there are infinitely more people in Hell than in Heaven.

I have not to believe that, and I do not believe it. Yet I believe in Christianity. Why should you, a non-Christian, prescribe for me what I have to believe? You might at least leave that to Christians.

34. Are Judas and Adam in Hell?

It has never been revealed that any particular soul is in Hell. Christ said of Judas, "Better for him had he never been born." Matt. XXVI, 24. That does not look too hopeful in his case, for no matter what a man has to endure, if he attains eternal happiness in the end, much better for him to have been born. However, even of Judas, no man has absolute certainty. The question can be solved only by God. It is practically certain that Adam is in Heaven, and not in Hell. Thus Scripture says, "Wisdom preserved him that was formed by God, the father of the world . . . and brought him out of his sin." Wisd. X, 1-2. Adam was the type of the second Adam, Christ, and it is to be expected that Christ, the second Adam, would see to it that the first Adam was fully liberated from Satan. The Greek Church from very ancient times, has celebrated the feast of Adam and Eve.

35. Why does the Church offer us Hell when we have Hell on earth?

The Church offers Hell to no one. She does all she can to prevent people from going there. Meantime Hell is not in this life. Those in Hell are irrevocably lost, and no one is irrevocably lost while still in this life. Until his very last breath every man has the opportunity offered him to save his soul. Nor are the ills and sufferings of this life Hell. They are often a very good medicine, curing us of over-attachment to this earthly life. Again, Christ our Lord endured more bitter sufferings during life than others are called upon to endure, and in no way could He be regarded as experiencing contact with Hell.

36. Where is Hell?

It is a state of suffering awaiting men after death, if they fail to depart this life in the grace and friendship of God. Information concerning its locality has not been revealed in terms of longitude and latitude, even could such terms avail. God has revealed that there is a Hell, but not where it is. And the latter information is immaterial, nor can any argument be based upon its absence. If the cables reported an earthquake at Potosi, your ignorance of the locality of Potosi would not disprove the earthquake. Our not knowing where Hell is makes no difference whatever to Hell. God has told us that it is a reality and that a man is a fool who does not fulfill the conditions necessary to avoid it.

37. Modern progressive scientific theology has no time for Hell.

The idea that there is no Hell is neither progressive nor scientific. It is not progressive, for it is not progress to leave people ignorant of a chasm yawning beneath their feet. If to take the truth from people and leave them in error be progress, then only could you call this progress. Nor is it scientific. There is not a jot of evidence that there is no eternal Hell, whilst God says that there is one. The men who deny Hell go by their feelings, shutting their eyes to facts. No scientist does that. I feel that there ought not to be a cancer. But there is a cancer.

38. Many pretend to believe and are hypocrites.

Very few would pretend to believe in Hell. An immense number pretend to themselves that they do not believe, and they do so in order to carry on as tranquilly as possible in evil conduct. Those who want to suppress Hell are not characterized by a real desire to defend the honor of God, to be more scrupulous in the observance of His laws, and to be more faithful in the fulfillment of their duties.

39. Believers' lives must be overshadowed by stupendous horror!

There is no reason why that should be at all. They have only to repent of their sins sincerely and resolve to avoid grave violations of conscience, which alone can lead to Hell. It is the man who does those things which God strictly forbids who has reason to be overshadowed, and even he by the horror of his conduct chiefly, and secondarily, by the prospect of the fate such conduct deserves.

40. Where this terrible dogma does not embitter happiness, it destroys character.

That is a gratuitous assertion. I believe in Hell. Since it exists I would much rather know than not know. And the knowledge does not embitter my happiness. As for my corrupt character, you at least have not sufficient evidence to judge me on that point.

41. If I could rob people of their faith in Hell I should not feel any regret.

That is because you do not understand the Christian religion, nor the nature of the eternal moral law. Hell exists, and since it does exist, it is treason to the God of truth and treachery to man to try to blind men to the fact.

42. Treachery to man! Are you pleased to know that there is a Hell?

Since there is one, I am glad to know it. I do not want to think that there is not a Hell if there is one. And I am glad that there is a Hell. I am glad that the state has penalties attached to the breaking of its laws. If there were no such penalties, its laws would fail to preserve the peace and well-being of the community as they should. In the same way I am glad that God has a deterring penalty attached to the violation of His Commandments.

43. Is your desire of Hell for your fellowmen due to your humanitarian sentiment or to the effete doctrine of your infallible Church?

I do not desire Hell for my fellowmen. I desire to save them from it. A truly humanitarian sentiment makes me glad that evil conduct is not a matter of indifference. It would be a dreadful thing if all men thought that they could sin with impunity. Your talk of an effete doctrine of an infallible Church is absurd.

44. I am human, and I can't believe in a burning Hell, above all for souls Christ came to redeem.

I cannot believe that Christ came to redeem people if there be no Hell from which to redeem them. But beware of your imagination. If you imagine a Hell which is in any way opposed to the justice and love of God, that is not the Hell you are asked to believe in at all. God is just, merciful, and truthful. He says that there is a Hell, and you are asked to believe in the Hell which He knows to exist, not in any vague speculation of your own as to its nature. Hell is as much a mystery of faith as is grace, and you are asked to believe in the fact of Hell because God knows the truth and could not tell an untruth. You are not asked to comprehend fully its nature, and your inability to believe in the Hell you imagine does not mean that you are unable to believe in the Hell which God created for "the devil and his angels."

45. How could a mother be happy in Heaven with her child in Hell?

She could not were her view of things limited by her present inadequate ideas. But with an unclouded view of what really constitutes goodness and of what really constitutes evil, she will have very different estimates in Heaven which will render happiness not only possible but a fact. Let us try to grasp it. Hell being a fact, our lack of understanding makes no difference. And in any case, Christ loved the child more than did the mother herself, yet He is happy in Heaven. So there must be some way out. You see, we cannot interpret Heaven in terms of this life. Here we are natural beings, our natural love directly awakened by our fellow beings. But in Heaven God Himself will be the direct object of our love. We shall love God, what God loves, and as God loves. All other beings will be loved in God. Thus Christ said concerning the difference of human love in Heaven that marriage shall not exist, but that men will be "as the angels of God in Heaven." Matt. XXII., 30. Merely natural love will change to supernatural love in and through God, and people will be lovable insofar as they resemble God. If a son dies unrepentant, having identified himself with wickedness. then he will be the opposite of God. The mother will experience an absolute necessity to love God who is pure, just, holy, and truth itself. And she will find complete happiness in doing so. Her natural love for her son gives way to a supernatural love for him if he is pure, just, holy and truthful. But it gives way to her love for God if her child is impure, unjust, wicked and essentially a liar, as is the father of lies himself. Her transfer to Heaven has changed her reasons for loving her son, and if he dies in such evil dispositions she has no supernatural reason to love him.

All her happiness is in God, and that happiness cannot be disturbed. This may sound difficult. It must. For we are trying to explain conditions of Heaven by ideas drawn from our earthly experience, ideas which do not go far enough. The explanation gives a solution as far as the limited mind of man can go. And if it astonishes human reason, we should be more astonished still if our limited powers could fully grasp the matter.

46. Is any person so bad as to deserve eternal punishment?

Yes. The man who deliberately and finally despises and rejects the Infinite Love of God deserves to be deprived of it forever.

47. Surely he did some virtuous actions. Are they to be of no avail?

They would have counted for very much, had the man wished. But if he subsequently commits mortal sin and dies without repenting of it he forfeits any benefits of previous virtue. Refraining from adultery on Friday is no excuse for the commission of murder on Saturday.

48. You damn people whose wills are so weak that they cannot avoid sin.

None but deliberately willed and unrepented mortal sin meets with eternal punishment. If inherent weakness is so great as to destroy real responsibility, God would not accuse man of mortal sin. But such is not the case with the normal man. The normal man is able to refuse consent of the will to evil inclinations and suggestions. Some people are only too ready to call their own cowardice inherent weakness. They could have refused to sin, and afterwards fell back on the lame excuse of "weak moments."

49. However bad people may be, I think it is against the right ideas of God to speak of His punishing anyone forever.

Then what are you going to do with Satan? He is a creature of God even as we. Is he going to reform? Will he ever come out of the eternal fire prepared for the devil and his angels? No. And granting the fact that God is punishing one of His creatures like that, responsible human souls can certainly meet with the same fate. I do not like the thought of anyone suffering in Hell any more than you do. But that will not make me deny the existence of Hell. Hundreds of things we do not like are facts.

50. That any human being should be sent to such a Hell of misery as you have described seems to me a monstrous injustice.

Far from its being an injustice, justice demands a Hell. All law has a sanction, and, to be efficacious, the sanction must be proportionate to the malice of the criminal. "No sanction, no law," is an axiom. It is absurd to say, "You must do this," if you have to reply to the query, "What if I do not, what will happen?" by weakly saying, "Oh, nothing!" Justice is a principle. Human justice demands sanctions. Flaunt the law; deliberately take somebody's life, and the due penalty is incurred. But if human justice fails to apprehend a criminal, God will not fail to balance the scales of justice. Then, too, many crimes against the law of God, and against conscience, are outside human jurisdiction. But God is not mocked. And serious, unrepented sin will meet with the irrevocable penalty of an eternal living death. The soul, immortal of its very nature, cannot but survive; and it will live on forever either as the friend of God or at enmity with God. But consider the position. God manifests His serious laws. If there be no eternal retribution, a soul can cry to Him, "Oh, I know You can punish me for a time, but even You will be **obliged** to pardon me, to make me happy in the end. There's no eternal punishment. Then let it all come. I care nothing for Your laws, nor shall I ever repent of having flung down the gauntlet to You. Do Your worst. I'm going to do as I like and pay no attention to any of Your rights over me." I simply ask, would justice be satisfied if God had to pardon such a creature of His own making? The compulsory pardon of such a creature would be to lie at the thing's feet, insulted and trampled upon forever. No. Justice demands eternal retribution for those who knowingly and deliberately flout God's laws and choose not to repent of having done so.

51. I still maintain that it is unjust to be punished eternally for a sin which occupied but a few moments.

In our own world life-sentences are given for crimes of perhaps two minutes' duration; and no one calls it unjust. The punishment is not proportionate to the time a sin takes, but to its gravity, malice and sheer wickedness.

52. Where is this enormous gravity in eating meat on Friday, which the Catholic Church regards as a mortal sin? Hell for such a trifle is outrageous.

The soul would not be punished simply for the eating of meat on Friday. It would be punished for violating a grave law of the Catholic Church. The grave law forbidding meat on Fridays takes its significance, not from the thing forbidden, but from the divine authority behind the law, and a deliberate defiance of the authority of God, certainly a mortal sin. It is a case of radical obedience or disobedience. The law is that one cannot have a given pleasure and the friendship of God. If one says, "Well, I prefer this particular pleasure to the friendship of God," takes the pleasure, and dies without repenting, God can only say, "You can't reject my friendship and have it." Christ said to the Church, "Whatever you bind on earth shall be bound in Heaven." Mt. XVIII, 18. Now, the Church binds Catholics under pain of mortal sin not to eat meat on Friday. Christ gave up His life in frightful suffering on that day, and the Church commands Catholics, as an act of grateful remembrance and in a spirit of obedience, to give up the pleasure of taking meat. And as Christ said of His Church, "He that hears you hears Me, and he that despises you despises Me." Lk. X, 16. Catholics know that to despise the authority of their Church in this matter is to despise Christ. You see, you have not understood the real character of the sin. To despise and reject Christ is to despise and reject an infinite good. Infinite punishment is proportionate.

53. Do you mean to say that even sixty years of sin would not be expiated by ten times sixty years of suffering and misery?

If a man renounced his sins, repudiated his evil dispositions, and turned to God in repentant love, much less might suffice to wipe out his debts. All depends upon the intensity with which he loves God at the moment of death. A very great love of God can fully expiate past sins. Thus Christ said, "Many sins are forgiven her because she has loved much." Lk. VII, 47. And it is a fact that God has often been most tenaciously loved by those who at one time offended him most. But if a man dies in a state of grave and unrepented mortal sin, ten times sixty years would certainly not suffice to wipe out his debt to God. He died without renouncing his evil dispositions. His time of probation is over. He dies identified with sin. He neither can, nor does he wish to change. Did he get the chance, he would commit the same sins again. His malice is a persevering debt never expiated, but concurrently renewed in the midst of his suffering. A life of sixty years in sin, taken by itself, could be expiated, provided it had been repudiated, and the will were not persevering in malicious opposition to God. But if a man has never retracted his evil will, the debt can never be wiped out. It's not a question of past sinful actions over and done with. It's a question of an everpresent disposition of malice irreconcilable with God.

54. Happily, for all your talk of a sufficient sanction, our present emotions are too strong to be influenced by hazy thoughts of the next life.

As thousands of people resist strong emotional attractions precisely because of their convictions concerning the next life, your statement is untrue. Our emotions are not too strong to allow us to be influenced by thoughts of the next life. I grant that many people refuse to think and ponder over the reality of the next life and deliberately allow their emotions to sway and even usurp the place of reason—not, however, happily.

55. Your dry logic of just sanctions leaves me unimpressed. God is a God of goodness, love, and mercy.

God's very goodness and love demand Hell for the wicked, and mercy cannot be invoked on behalf of one who deliberately rejects it. Part of God's goodness is His very justice. His perfections are in perfect harmony and cannot contradict each other. In fact, a denial of Hell is a denial of God's goodness and holiness. Were He less holy, Hell might not be eternal. But the holier God is, the greater His aversion to sin. His infinite love also demands Hell for those who reject it. Love and hatred go together. If we are indifferent to a thing, we do not resent its destruction. But the more one loves good, the more one resents the evil which would destroy the good. The divine spirit of love is the everlasting reward of the holy yet the undying hatred which will forever enkindle the flames of Hell. It is not so difficult to understand. When the white light of the sun falls upon an object which absorbs the light, it appears white. If it reflects some of the light, it appears colored. So, when the love of God bestows being upon a rational creature, if the will absorbs all to itself and reflects none of that love to the honor and glory of God, the soul renders itself black in God's sight, and His hatred is the result of His very love. "If I exist at all," the soul could say, "it is because of God's love. I cannot say why His love wished me to exist, but I can say why He hates me." Let us remember, too, that the love of God prompted the incarnation of His only-begotten Son, the greatest act of love yet; and if sin was bad enough to warrant the incarnation and death of the Son of God, it is bad enough to warrant Hell for those who despise the means offered for their redemption.

56. But I cannot bring myself to believe that a God of love would condemn a soul to everlasting suffering.

In a way you are quite right, but not in the way you think. A God of love supposes a God who does love, and that supposes an object loved. If a soul is the object of God's love, that soul will not be condemned to Hell. But God is good, and loves what is good. Loving what is good, He must hate what is evil He, therefore, hates the moral evil called sin. That is why He forbids sin. If, then, a soul identifies itself with sin, it identifies itself with the object of God's hatred. There is no God of love for that soul whilst, and insofar as, it clings to its evil dispositions. If a soul dies without disassociating itself from evil by repentance, it will go to Hell. But it is not sent there by a God of love; it is rejected by the God of justice. You seem to think that a God of love must love everything, whether good or evil. That is not true. God is a God of love in the sense that He must love all that is good. If I am good, He is a God of love to me. If I am evil, I forfeit any claim to His love. As long as we identify ourselves with that moral goodness which God can love, He is a God of love to us, and we cannot be lost. In that sense, the God of love never condemns a soul to everlasting punishment. But the evil soul who forfeits God's love will certainly meet with that fate.

57. Don't you think that cruelty is the most hateful vice?

It is not the most hateful vice, but it is thoroughly evil and a form of savage brutality. However, the doctrine of Hell does not justify in any way the attributing of cruelty to God.

58. He who sentences even the vilest creature to eternal torture is more cruel than the most cruel of men.

Cruelty is the infliction of punishment upon the innocent or beyond due measure upon the guilty. God is not cruel. He is just. When you mention cruelty, you unconsciously make appeal to the sentiment of human pity. Now, we pity involuntary evils. We pity the one who suffers involuntarily. We pity criminals who repent and try to make good. We pity them even before they repent if we feel that there is yet hope that they may do so. But we do not pity the man who hardens himself in his evil intentions—won't repent, but tells us that he is going on with his malicious practices, no matter what we say. A mother who does not know how to punish does not know how to pity her child. Weakness leads to impunity. And remember that God sends no one to Hell. Men go there. God does not want them to go there, otherwise His warning us that there is a Hell would be absurd.

59. One who believes in Hell cannot understand the horrible nature of the vice of cruelty, not fearing to cast a reflection on God.

I believe in the existence of Hell. I am not in the least likely to regard that doctrine as implying cruelty in God, nor do I think I have a lower estimate of the horrible nature of cruelty than you. The God I serve abominates it, and will punish willful and serious and unrepented cruelty to one's fellows by Hell forever. Even you don't hate it that much.

60. God should set a good example to men.

He does so. Your complaint is that He manifests too great a love for the good and too great a corresponding hatred of evil. You want Him to sanction evil, and tell men that He doesn't mind so very much if they do sin.

61. It is an outrage on Christian sympathy to all who realize what Hell really is.

What Hell really is, will never be realized by human intelligence in this life. The fact that there is a Hell is known because God has revealed its existence. And is it an outrage on Christian sympathy to think that God's strict rights will be vindicated? If a man **has any** Christian sympathy, it goes out to Christ above all, dying in great suffering upon the cross precisely to save men of good will from the eternal punishment of Hell – and he does **not** sympathize with those who blaspheme and despise Christ, and fling back into God's face this love-offering of His own Son. No man can deliberately reject God's love and have it.

62. You talk of injustice, but you seem to have forgotten the mercy of God.

I have not forgotten the mercy of God. But you have forgotten that mercy is begged for, not forced upon people against their will. God will mercifully pardon anything, on sincere repentance; nothing without it. There is room for pardon, but not for impunity.

63. But how could a merciful God send anyone to Hell?

God sends no one to Hell. Fools go there. God warns us against Hell very seriously. If He wished us to go there, the last thing He would do would be to warn us against it.

But none of these difficulties can avail against the fact. As surely as good and evil exist in this world, so do their counterparts in eternity—Heaven and Hell. And, above all, since God has said that there is a Hell, there is no use in urging our ideas as to whether there should be one or not. It is better to give our attention to the living of a life which cannot end in Hell. As Fr. Rickaby has pointed out, "There is only one way to abolish Hell; abolish your own by a good life."

64. Would it not be better not to create, than to punish some soul forever in Hell?

Even did that seem better to us, our little ideas are not in the measure of all that is truly wise. Creation is a fact. Hell is a fact. That souls can be lost is a fact. If we find it hard to reconcile these facts with our human ideas, we can only conclude that our ideas must be limited and inadequate, and that God's infinite wisdom must percieve more aspects than those to which we advert. God has, in fact, revealed this truth in the words, "My thoughts are not your thoughts, nor your ways My ways." We are too prone to concentrate on individual details and lose sight of the whole scheme. God has not to choose between creating this or that individual, but He made a race of beings propagating its kind. And He saw that the general good far outweighed the individual losses. After all, if my great-grandfather lost his soul, that would be his own fault. There was no need for him to do so. But if he had not been allowed to exist, my grandfather, my father, and myself would not have had the opportunity of saving our souls. There is no reason why I should be deprived of eternal happiness (if I attain it) because my great-grandfather chose to throw away his eternal happiness (if he did). A complete solution of the difficulty, of course, cannot be given. Man's powers of comprehension are very limited. But reason can at least show that objections proposed by reason are not valid, and it can also show that wild conclusions and denials go far beyond any of the evidence that can be advanced in their favor.

65. The future has no real bearing on morality, and if anything, would have a bad influence, making men cowards.

Since there is a future life, it has a lot to do with morality. Man is endowed with reason and is bound to exercise foresight. The future as such, whether here or hereafter, is a reasonable motive for present conduct. I refrain from eating certain foods now, because reason tells me that future indigestion will result. That is reasonable conduct. I try to refrain from morally wrong conduct because it is wrong; offends God; is a personal disgrace; and will wreck my whole future existence if I persist in it, dying without repentance. All these motives are good. If the nobler motives fail to impress me in a given temptation, the thought of hell at least will tend to stop me.

You will say, "So you are afraid of hell?" I reply, "Of course I am!" Knowing that hell is a reality, any sane man will live so as to avoid going there. It is not cowardice, but ordinary prudence. If a man leaps for his life off a railway line as an express train tears past the spot where he was standing, you would not go up to him, tap him on the shoulder, and say, "You coward, you jumped for your life through sheer fear of that train!" God gave us our reason that we might use it for our well-being, and it is quite reasonable to weigh both advantages and penalties attached to moral law.

Nor is this influence probably to the bad. The knowledge that retribution will follow violations of the moral law makes that law a real law. Could we say that all the penalties attached to the laws of the State are to the bad? Thousands of temptations to crime are resisted by citizens because of the thought of the future penalties. Nor does it matter much whether the penalty be future by a few weeks and in this life, or by some years, and in the next life. The principle is the same.

66. Has not rationalism made havoc of Christianity, reducing the Bible to a myth, and quenching the fires of hell by humanitarian principles?

It has not made havoc of Christianity. It is making havoc of Protestantism. But Protestantism is not really Christianity. The Catholic Church alone is the true representative of Christianity, and she is not affected by rationalism. The Bible is as authentic as ever, and humanitarianism has not affected the **fires of hell**, even as it had nothing to do with their creation. As has been well said, the only way to **abolish hell** is to abolish one's own by leading a good life, and serving God.

67. How does Protestantism in general disobey Christ?

In general it says that Scripture is a sufficient guide to salvation, although Scripture says that it is not; it denies the authority of the Church established by Christ; it has no sacrifice of the Mass; it does not believe in confession;

it denies Christian teaching on marriage; it rejects Purgatory, and very often its advocates **refuse to believe in hell** But I could go on almost forever. Meantime, if you give me any doctrine taught by one Protestant Church, I will produce another Protestant Church which denies it, save perhaps the one doctrine that there is a God of some sort.

A RIGHT PERSPECTIVE

I have been dealing with isolated aspects of this whole question of hell, proposed as difficulties. But their very isolation destroys perspective. Firstly, it is a mistake to think that eternal things can be measured by ideas proper to finite men; and, secondly, it is a mistake to concentrate on individual attributes of God, such as His mercy, to the exclusion of all other attributes. As Leibuity, the non-Catholic philosopher, has remarked, "We know next to nothing of God's ways, and to wish to measure His wisdom and goodness with our finite ideas is absurd temerity." And our separation of God's attributes is not justified for purposes of objection. We must take all in their general connection, balancing one with another, and seeing each as the reason of the others. God is not just, and also good, and also merciful. He is justice, goodness, mercy. In the supreme unity of God these are one. It is the feebleness of our intelligence which suggests separation in these divine attributes. If hell, then, is demanded by God's justice, it is demanded by His goodness and mercy also. And if a soul is lost, it is allowed to lose itself both by God's justice and mercy.

Difficulties are bound to arise for us. But objections against the doctrine of hell are not justified; for he who objects supposes the doctrine of hell to be false. And that gives the lie to God, who has revealed hell to be a fact.

CONCLUSION

There is a hell. The idea of eternal suffering may not appeal. It does not appeal to me. Yet hell is a fact, nevertheless. A terrible doom awaits the finally impenitent, and it is well to remember it. And the thought of hell should at least teach us the gravity of sin. Fire gives light. Let the fire of hell give us this light. And let it harden our endurance that we may face any trial and difficulty rather than sin. "Here cut, here burn," cried St. Augustine, "but spare me in eternity." This life is the time of our probation, and death is the end of hope for him who dies radically opposed to God. "If it were justice alone," writes Lacordaire, "which has prepared the abyss, there would have been a remedy. But it is love also, and this it is which takes away all hope. When we are condemned by justice, we may have recourse to love; but when we are condemned by love, to whom shall we have recourse? Such is the lot of the damned. They have tried love too far. It is life or death; and when there is question of the love of a God, it is eternal life, or eternal death."

These are the thoughts which lend weight, indeed, to Our Lord's words, "What shall it profit a man if he gain the whole world and lose his soul?" For loss of one's soul means hell, and for all eternity. This is not a thought with which we may trifle. It is basic in Christianity, and alone explains the passionate desire to save souls so evident in the apostles of Christ throughout the ages. And the salvation of our own souls is equally a matter of urgent necessity. Sin must be renounced, and God must be served. "Man with his free will," says Fr. Rickaby, "may in this life defy God; but it will not be forever. God deals with man fairly, never asking back what He has not first given to man. Nay, God deals with man mercifully, allowing, even entreating, him to take back false moves. But any one false move, in downright defiance of God, may be the last move of the game. God may foreclose the mortgage of life at any moment, and it is a fearful thing to fall into the hands of the living God. Your will strongly bent in opposition to His! The outcome of such a conflict and collision with an Almighty Being is beyond the power of reason to calculate.

Augustine Joseph Roth, a former Baptist minister, tells the story of his conversion in booklet, "Out of the Wilderness," Sunday Visitor, in answer to critics:

Among the many letters I received from former friends in the Protestant ministry, after it became known that I was to be received into the Catholic Church, was one from Dr. Wallace Sharpe, an instructor of a seminary that I had attended. I do not question the sincerity that prompted my preceptor to write me; however, there is one part of his letter that cannot go unchallenged. If Dr. Sharpe is sincere, he is absolutely ignorant of what he writes, and I sincerely hope that this article will enlighten him for the future. I quote part of his letter:

"You have not been fair with yourself in this matter. Instead of going to impartial sources for information, you went to a Catholic priest, and instead of an impartial informant you found a fox only too willing to praise the beauty of his own tail. I dare say that had you gone to other men of intelligence, not necessarily Baptists, you would have met so very different a story, that you could not, conscientiously, become a Catholic. The entire student body agrees on this."

I believe that I was a fairly intelligent non-Catholic of the kind my former professor has reference to; and had any Protestant come to me to learn something about the Catholic Church, I would have given him the so-called intelligent argument. Somewhere I had read "The Awful Disclosures of Maria Monk." Elsewhere I had read "Thirty Years in Hell," by one who repudiated his book before he died; and at another time I wasted good time on a volume entitled "Crimes Against the Jesuits." Fortified with this abundant supply of knowledge of the Catholic Church, I set out to warn the unsuspecting of the dangers of Catholicism. I had personally purchased and distributed no less than a hundred copies of Maria Monk and perhaps as many of the others. Whenever I was asked anything about the Catholic Church, I tipped back on my heels and swelled up like a pouter pigeon, for I considered myself a living encyclopedia and the source of all information about the Catholics. At the end of my discourse, I gave the inquirer a copy of one of these books, and strutted off like a peacock, honestly believing that I had accomplished something worth while.

For years I followed this method of dealing intelligently in regards to the Catholic Church, and regardless of my sincerity, I am sure that I turned back many an honest seeker of the Truth. It is impossible to estimate the number of Protestant ministers, using this same method of **intelligently** instructing others concerning the Catholic Church, and who are keeping others from the joy of the true Faith.

Their Sincerity Is Not Questioned

The sincerity of these men does not help matters one iota. I have often heard these words: "Oh, well, they are sincere;" and I cannot find it in myself to condone such sincerity any more than I can condone the sincerity of the thief who steals the savings of the widow and orphan. My own brother, a well-known Baptist minister, will have nothing whatever to do with me since I became a Catholic, claiming, as he does, that I have disgraced the family. My own sister, a prominent business woman of New York, will not so much as answer a letter, charging me, as she does, with bringing shame on her by becoming a Catholic. Sincere? No doubt; but a sincerity bred of bigotry and hatred is not to be respected. A man may be quite sincere, and yet be quite wrong, just as wrong as I was in taking to heart the sinful lies of the infamous "Maria Monk"—and just as wrong, as I shall attempt to prove in this phamphlet, as my former professor is in believing that non-Catholic men and women of intelligence, are sure to speak ill of the Catholic Church.

Nor does it necessarily follow that because the faculty and the entire student body agree in what Dr. Sharpe says, that it must be so. I agree that the majority rules, but I do not agree that the majority is always right. Let me give one illustration in this respect. Yonder in prison is Barabbas; here stands Christ. Now which shall it be: Thief, murderer, inciter of riots, or, Jesus the Saviour of Men, the Prince of Peace? The majority cry "release Barabbas and crucify Christ." The voice of the rabble, the majority, carried that day, but, who today will admit that the majority was right? In your own student body there are Methodists who think you are wrong; there are Presbyterians who think you are both wrong; there are Campbellites who think the three of you are wrong. You cannot agree among yourselves on hardly one point of Christian doctrine, but you are all united in one thing, that I am wrong because I became a Catholic.

Fair-Minded Ministers Agree

You claim that I should have gone to non-Catholics for my information about Catholics but, the Rev. J. B. Hemmeon, a Methodist minister, does not agree with you, for he says:

"It is a strange and lamentable fact that not one Protestant in ten thousand knows the truth about the teaching and practice of the Catholic Church. Many do not know there was any other Christian Church from the first or second century until the 'Reformation,' or for about one thousand four hundred years. And they believe that there was then, virtually, a new Revelation.

"When a person of common sense wishes to obtain information about anything, whether political, religious, scientific, or it matters not what it may be, he goes to headquarters for authentic information—never to those who seek to destroy, or who are the enemies of that which he wishes to study. Not one Protestant in thousands ever seeks information concerning the Catholic Church from Catholic sources. The history from the Apostles to the fifteenth century is not taught in any Protestant seminary, nor anywhere else amongst Protestants, as far as I know. Nor is it possessed by

Protestants . . . I studied theology, passed my examinations for the Methodist Church, and knew absolutely nothing of Christianity, or whether there was any, during this period. When I awoke to the fact of my dense ignorance, I felt resentment; and I confess I do to this day."

Nor is Dr. Hemmeon alone in his opinion. Says Dr. Washington Gladden, a Congregationalist of Columbus, Ohio:

"Among non-Catholics, even men of education are woefully ignorant of the Catholic Church."

And Dr. Nightengale, a Methodist, in his, "Religions of All Nations," has this to say:

"In scarcely a single instance has a case concerning them (Catholics) been fairly stated; the channels of history, not grossly corrupted."

But it is not my wish to show you how many men of intelligence among the non-Catholic clergy, disagree with you. I wish to show you and those who share your opinion, that non-Catholics of intelligence, have been most outspoken in their praise of the Catholic Church, and that Protestant ministers and well-known laymen, have been most outspoken in voicing their disapproval of the Protestant Church. Let us hear what informed non-Catholics have to say.

Well-Informed Ministers Speak Out

Rev. A. M. Courtney, a Methodist, of Chillicothe, Ohio:

"If I could destroy the Catholic Church tomorrow as easily as I could turn over my hand I should not do so, for it has a great mission to perform and it performs it as the Protestant Church could not do. It finds a place for every person, be he the religious enthusiast, the worker for mercy, the distributor of charity, or the recluse. It places these persons where they may do the most good, and that the Protestant Church does not do. Its writers and theologians, Thomas Aquinas, for instance, are the font of inspiration to all Christianity and its organization is the most perfect in existence. The Protestant Church owes all that is best in it to the Catholic Church."

Rev. T. B. Thompson, Congregationalist minister of Chicago, Ill.:

"To contemplate her history is to admire her. Reformations, wars, empires, and kingdoms have been arrayed against her. After all these centuries she stands so strong and so firmly rooted in the lives of millions that she commands our highest respect. As an institution she is the most splendid the world has ever seen. Governments have risen and gone to the grave of nations since her advent. Peoples of every tongue have worshipped at her altars . . . The Roman Catholic Church has stood solid for law and order . . . When she speaks, legislators, statesmen, politicians, and governments stop to listen, often to obey. In the realm of worship her ministry has been of the highest . . . her cathedrals are the shrines of all pilgrims."

Rev. James Benninger, a Methodist of Wilkes-Barre, Pa.:

"The reason the Catholic Church succeeds, in spite of our misgivings, is because she is true to the central fact of revelation. She makes the death of Jesus the center of her devotion, around that point she organizes all her activities. When you see a company of Catholic people on the way to church, you can be assured of this: they are not going for the sake of fine music; they are not going to hear an eloquent dissertation on 'Dr. Jekyl or Mr. Hyde.' They are going to that place of worship to attend Mass. What is the celebration of the Mass? It is what we call the celebration of the Lord's Supper. That fact is kept prominently before the mind of every Catholic. What is the first thing you see as you approach the Catholic Church? A cross. What is the first thing you see as you enter that church? A cross. What is the first thing you see a Catholic do as he seats himself in that church? Make the sign of a cross. What is the last thing held before the eyes of a dying Catholic? A cross. He comes into the Church in childhood imbued with the death of Jesus; he goes out of the world thinking of the death of Jesus."

Rev. Madison C. Peters, a Baptist minister of New York, N. Y.:

"Catholics teach us a lesson of constant attendance upon public worship. Protestants go when the weather is just to their liking. Who has not heard early on Sunday mornings the tramp, tramp, of people, with a hard week's work behind them, while we are asleep, hastening to the Catholic Church, with prayer book in hand? . . . Our religion is too much talk. We have too many women's meetings and not enough Sisters of Charity."

Rev. J. S. Thompson, Independent Church, Los Angeles, Cal.:

"The providential purpose of the Roman Church is unity and continuity. The Catholic Church is the grandest organization in the world. It has a place of consecrated duty for all types or groups of mind. The poor, the common, and the rich meet together in that Church, as children of the same common Father. The poor, hard-working man and woman are found in that Church. It is an ancient Church. It was the ancient Church before the birth of Protestantism. It has cohesion and unity and continuity. The very fact of its great age is proof of its providential purpose. It traces its descent to the founder of our common Christianity. The gates of Hades have not been able to destroy it. It stands today a victor over the opposition of centuries. It is the strongest religious force in Christendom."

Rev. Dr. T. Moffatt, a Congregationalist of Newark, N. J.: "What do I admire in the Catholic Church? There are seven things which the Protestant Church might imitate and which I admire in the Catholic Church, and they are these: First, emphasis of the sanctity of the marriage vow; second, the pomp and dignity and parade of the Church; third, the central unifying authority of the Church; fourth, the tone of conviction; fifth, femininity, as exemplified in the honor paid the Blessed Virgin Mary; sixth, purgatory; and lastly, confession."

Rev. B. P. Dimmick, a Methodist, of Columbus, Ohio: "For centuries the Roman Church was the only organized representation of Christianity in the world. During all this time she stood as a bulwark of defense against all foes that assaulted our holy Christianity. But for her, the Church of God would have perished from off the earth. During all the centuries of darkness and heathenism in the world, this Church preserved the essentials of the doctrines of Christianity. We have the fundamentals of Christian doctrine, such as belief in One True God and His Son, Jesus Christ, our Blessed Lord. A Church that has given the world the example of so many holy saints as the Roman Church has made a contribution to the uplift of the race that is incalculable."

Rev. N. Schuyler, Protestant Episcopal, of Trenton, N. J.: "Roman Catholicism lays great stress upon the performance of outward acts, while Protestantism affects to make light of such things. In this attitude I am firmly convinced that Roman Catholicism is right and Protestantism wholly wrong. A genuine religion must manifest itself in some outward way."

Non-Catholic Laymen Also Speak Fairly

So far I have quoted only non-Catholic ministers. The list is not exhausted by far, but space will not permit more here. However, there are others who have been no less outspoken and among these are:

The Late Senator (Mark) Hanna:

"There is a crisis coming which will have to be met and the sooner the better. There is no place in this country, for anarchy and treason. In this connection I once said that in the day of trouble the United States must look to the Supreme Court and to the Roman Catholic Church. I will go further now and say that I believe the best friend and protector the people and the flag shall have in its hour of trial will be the Roman Church, always conservative and fair and loyal. This is the power that shall save us."

John D. Rockefeller, writing in "World's Work," says:

"I fully appreciate the splendid service done by others in the field, but I have seen the organization of the Roman Catholic Church secure better results with a given sum of money than any other church organizations are accustomed to secure from the same expenditures."

The Hon. Stanley Matthews of the Superior Court of Cincinnati, O.:

"I will say that from the study which I have made, as time and opportunity have given me, of the doctrinel basis of the Roman Catholic Church, I am bound to say that it is not an ignorant superstitution, but a scheme of well-conducted logic, which he is a bold man who says he can easily answer. Give them one proposition, concede to them one single premise and the whole of their faith follows most legitimately and logically."

The Hon. W. E. Gladstone:

The Catholic Church has marched for more than fifteen hundred years at the head of human civilization; and has harnessed to her chariot, as the horses of a triumphal car, the chief intellectual and material forces of the world."

Nathaniel Hawthorne:

"I have always envied the Catholics in that sweet, sacred Virgin Mother who stands between them and the Diety; intercepting somewhat of His awful splendor, but permitting His love to stream on the worshipper more intelligibly to human comprehension through the medium of a woman's tenderness."

Oliver Wendell Holmes:

"So far as I have observed persons nearing the end of life, the Roman Catholics understand the business of dying better than Protestants. I have seen a good many Roman Catholics on their deathbeds and it always appeared to me that they accept the inevitable with composure which showed that their belief, whether or not the best to live by, was a better one to die by than most of the harder ones that have replaced it."

The great metaphysician, Heine, in his "Confessions," says:

"I know too well my own intellectual caliber not to be aware that, with my most furious onslaughts, I could inflict but little injury on such a Colossus as the Church of St. Peter. Many a new recruit will break his head against its walls. As a thinker, a metaphysician, I was always forced to pay the homage of my admiration to the logical consistency of the doctrines of the Roman Catholic Church."

Even Renan, writing from Rome in 1849, says:

"I came to this country singularly prejudiced against the religion of the south. I had in my mind set phrases as to this sensual, unwholesome, and subtle worship. To me Rome was the perversion of the religious instinct. I intended to ridicule freely the permanental ingenuity of the Church of Christ and of the superstitious of this land. Well, my friend, the Madonna has conquered me.